The GHOST of BRACKEN HILL

ANNE MACKINTOSH

Illustrated by Tony Morris

OXFORD
UNIVERSITY PRESS

OXFORD
UNIVERSITY PRESS

Great Clarendon Street, Oxford OX2 6DP

Oxford University Press is a department of the University of Oxford.
It furthers the University's objective of excellence in research, scholarship,
and education by publishing worldwide in

Oxford   New York

Auckland   Cape Town   Dar es Salaam   Hong Kong   Karachi
Kuala Lumpur   Madrid   Melbourne   Mexico City   Nairobi
New Delhi   Shanghai   Taipei   Toronto

With offices in

Argentina   Austria   Brazil   Chile   Czech Republic   France   Greece
Guatemala   Hungary   Italy   Japan   Poland   Portugal   Singapore
South Korea   Switzerland   Thailand   Turkey   Ukraine   Vietnam

Oxford is a registered trade mark of Oxford University Press
in the UK and in certain other countries

British Library Cataloguing in Publication Data
Data available

ISBN: 978-0-19-918427-9

17 19 20 18 16

Available in packs
Stage 15 Pack of 6:
ISBN: 978-0-19-918426-2
Stage 15 Class Pack:
ISBN: 978-0-19-918433-0
Guided Reading Cards also available:
ISBN: 978-0-19-918435-4

Cover artwork by Tim Clarey

Printed in Malaysia by
MunSang Printers Sdn Bhd

Paper used in the production of this book is a natural, recyclable product
made from wood grown in sustainable forests. The manufacturing process
conforms to the environmental regulations of the country of origin.

1

On the move again

'Letter for Dad,' I said. I put the envelope on the caravan table and Mum picked it up.

'Oh! What can she want!'

I looked at Mum. Her face went white as she snatched up the envelope.

'Who?' I asked.

'Great Aunt Sarah, your dad's aunt.' She put the envelope down again.

'She must be dead old then.'

'Well, she's not,' said Mum.

I could see she wasn't really listening to me.

Dad came in from the farm office. He picked up the letter, slit open the envelope and began to read. 'Well I never!' he exclaimed.

'What does she want after all these years?' Mum's voice sounded hoarse, as if she had difficulty speaking.

'Aunt Sarah wants us to come back to Ardcardish – to manage the shop for her. She says she's too old now.'

'You'll not go.' Mum made it sound like a statement, not a question.

'We'll see. Here, you read it for yourself, and we'll talk about it later on.'

I knew what that meant. They didn't want me to hear. It also meant that we might well be on the move again.

* * *

By the time I got home from school, I'd almost forgotten about the letter.

I slept in the kitchen part of the caravan, so I kept the window open that night.

4

The rain coming in through the window
woke me up, and I knelt in the bed to close
it. It was then I heard my parents talking.

'I don't want to go back,' I heard Mum say.

'I think we must. When Aunt Sarah dies, the shop will be mine. Tricia will get the post office. We're her only relatives. It'll be all right, you'll see. She wants to forget all the rows.'

'It's not that. It's the other thing. I don't want to go back – please, Jack, please.' Mum sounded desperate. I'd never heard her like that before, and I didn't like it.

'It's only an old tale. It'll be all …'

'But I've seen …'

'Helen, don't worry. Everything will work out. Let's get some sleep.'

I heard Dad switching off the light. The rain was heavy and it drummed on the metal roof of the caravan. I couldn't get back to sleep. I lay there thinking.

I knew the name Ardcardish. I knew we had lived there when I was small. Dad's sister, my Aunt Tricia, was the postmistress. Her husband, my Uncle Hamish, was dead; drowned some months ago. Her children, William and Margaret, were my cousins.

Somewhere from the back of my mind, came a picture of a building with stairs and green railings leading up to a long landing. And a dog. There was a dog somewhere.

I fell asleep and dreamed of a proper house with no kipper smells and a dog howling.

The following morning I asked Dad, 'Are we going to move again?' We had moved about quite a lot and I'd been to four different schools. I didn't want to move yet again.

'Yes, in a while.' I heard Mum draw in her breath sharply. She was making the breakfast.

Dad left for work, but I had time to help clear up before going to school.

'We lived in Ardcardish before, didn't we?' I said to Mum.

'We did.' She picked up two cups and turned to the sink.

'We lived in a house with green railings and a big landing. And we had a dog that often howled.'

Mum dropped the cups with a clatter and they bounced on the floor. She half turned towards me.

'We had no dog, Tom. There was no dog!' Her voice rose higher as she spoke. Her face had gone pale and her knuckles shone white as she gripped the sink edge.

'But Mum, I remem...'

'You don't remember! You can't remember –
you were only three when we left. That's
eight years ago!' She bent down to rescue the
two cups, and some of the colour came back
to her cheeks. 'Now get off to school.'

I hesitated. I'd never seen Mum in such a
state. I couldn't think why she was so upset.
She rushed me towards the door.

I grabbed my bag and coat and fled. I ran all the way down the lane to the main road. I puzzled over Mum's behaviour until the school bus arrived.

* * *

Letters passed between Dad and Aunt Sarah and Aunt Tricia. Dad talked to his boss, the farmer. Mum said very little; at least not to me.

* * *

On a miserable, wet Saturday in the middle of September, I said goodbye to my friends and we left to travel north to Scotland.

We stopped at a service station for lunch and I bought some comics to read. That didn't take me very long and I spent the rest of the journey dozing. I woke to find we were on a ferry, crossing a narrow strip of water. I sat up and looked round.

'Are we nearly there?'

'Yes, once we're off the ferry it's only a short way to the other end of the village.'

Mum was silent. She looked pale, as if she was scared. I really couldn't understand it. She had never been like this on any of our other moves.

'That's the school you'll be going to on Monday.' Mum pointed to a grey building as we drove past. 'Your dad went there when he was young.'

I looked out of the back window. The building looked forbidding in the fading light. Monday would come soon enough. Now I was about to meet Aunt Sarah, but not before I'd met my cousin, William.

2

Reunion

Dad turned into a yard behind a row of shops. As he stopped the car he tooted the horn. I looked up and there it was: the house that I remembered, with the green railings. I felt as if I had come home.

There were two doors; one was closed and the other open. Standing in the doorway under a bright landing light, was a rather plump lady with a small girl beside her.

Behind the girl, stood a boy with dark red hair like mine. I might have been looking at myself in the mirror.

Dad got out of the car, ran up the steps and hugged his sister. So that was my Aunt Tricia and the kids were my cousins, William and Margaret.

Mum got out of the car and went up the stairs to the landing. As I went up, I noticed a movement at one of the windows. I had the impression of someone with very white hair peering out – before the curtain dropped. It was so quick that I wondered if it had really happened.

Aunt Tricia hugged my mother and me. Margaret hid behind her mother, and William scowled. His scowl was spectacular, far worse than mine.

Aunt Tricia said, 'I've got a shepherd's pie nearly ready for you. Aunt Sarah has eaten. She'll see you tomorrow.' She opened the door to the other house and put on a hall light.

'Tom, do us a favour and bring up the two small bags,' said Dad, handing me the keys to the caravan.

'Give him a hand, William.' Aunt Tricia nudged him.

William and I went down the stairs in silence. I opened the caravan and was about to pick up my comics.

'I'll take these.' William grabbed the comics and turned to face me. 'She won't like you, you know!'

'What do you mean – who's "she"?'

'Aunt Sarah, of course – she won't like you,' William repeated.

'Why not? I've not even seen her since I was three.'

'Your name is Thomas. She doesn't like anyone called Thomas.'

'Well, she can call me by my middle name, David.'

'Won't make any difference. You'll see. You won't like it here either.' William prodded me with my comics. I tried to grab them, but he jerked away.

'Ask your mum – she knows what I mean.' He laughed as he jumped down the caravan steps, leaving me with the heavy bags.

I picked up the bags, locked the caravan and trudged back up the steps and into the house. I suddenly felt tired and miserable.

I'd hoped that William would be friendly, and now he'd pinched my comics!

In the kitchen, Mum was putting the pie on the table. Steam was rising from it. The top was crunchy brown, just the way I liked it. I felt a lot better.

After supper, Dad showed me my room.

'Which is Aunt Sarah's room?' I whispered.

'At the end of the corridor. It is the biggest room in the house and has windows looking out to the sea and the hill.'

Dad pointed to a door that was shut at the far end of the hall. A thin line of light could be seen under the door.

'She has her ways but she doesn't bite,' Dad said. 'You'll meet her in the morning.'

I went into my room and shut the door. I realized that Dad had been whispering too. I unpacked my pyjamas and got ready for bed. As I came back from the bathroom, I noticed there was no longer any light shining under Aunt Sarah's door.

3

What's she like?

The smell of bacon cooking woke me. Mum looked round as I came into the kitchen.

'Had a good sleep, Tom?' she asked and she put more bacon into the frying pan.

'Yes, thanks. Where's Dad?'

'He's talking to Aunt Sarah.' Mum put the plate down beside me. 'Start on that.'

'Have you seen her? What's she like?' I mumbled.

'Of course I have – and don't talk with your mouth full. She's very old and please don't bother her.'

Then Dad came in and Mum poured tea.

'She may be old but she's on the ball all right.' He picked up his cup and took a sip of tea. 'Tom, when you've finished your breakfast, Aunt Sarah wants to meet you.'

I finished eating and gulped down my tea. 'Come on then.'

I followed Dad. He knocked on Aunt Sarah's door and as he opened it he said, 'Here's Thomas to see you.'

I was startled. Dad hardly ever called me by my full name. He nudged me into the room and closed the door behind me.

'Come here, Thomas, where I can see you properly.'

All I could see was a hand waving at me from a high-backed chair beside the fire. I crossed the room and stood beside her. Her voice was strong and not at all what I'd imagined.

Aunt Sarah looked incredibly small in the big chair. She wore a black dress with a high collar, and a gold locket hung round her neck. A brightly-coloured rug hung over her knees. Her face was a mass of tiny lines and wrinkles, but her eyes, a sparkling blue, were bright and alert.

'Hello, Aunt Sarah.' I bent forward and shook her hand. Somehow, it seemed the right thing to do.

She may have been frail-looking but there was nothing frail about her handshake. I smiled at her, and resisted the urge to shake the blood back into my hand.

She looked me up and down without saying a word. I felt my face going red and was glad when she spoke.

'You are very like him, Thomas.' She smiled at me and I felt a bit better.

'Like who, Aunt Sarah?'

'My twin brother, Thomas, of course. You were given his name – against my wishes.'

She spoke quite fiercely.

I remembered what William had said the night before. I tried not to let my voice tremble.

'I thought I was named after my mum's own name, but my other name is David if you'd rather call me that.'

She really surprised me then.

She laughed; a great giggling sort of laugh
that bubbled up from her boots. She leaned
forward and touched my cheek.

'Don't worry, Thomas, you and I will get
on famously,' she grinned. 'Now go and ask
your mother if I can come and make my
elevenses soon.'

21

4

Old photos

Aunt Sarah had lunch with us that Sunday and she spent most of the time telling Dad how she wanted the shop to be run.

'And remember, Thomas, no going into the shop to take packets of crisps, or cans of that coke you young people drink. You pay for everything.' Aunt Sarah waved her stick in my direction as she was leaving the room.

'Yes, Aunt Sarah.'

Before she closed the door she turned. 'Why not join William and me this afternoon? We play chess.'

At three o'clock there was a knock on the door. 'Tom, here's William,' Mum called.

'I've come to play chess with Aunt Sarah, not to see *him*,' said William, in a grumpy voice.

'I know. But Aunt Sarah has invited Tom to play chess too.'

William scowled again but said nothing. We walked silently up the corridor to Aunt Sarah's room. Smiling mischievously, she let us in. William immediately set up a table beside her chair.

'Tom doesn't play chess,' he announced, 'so he can just watch.'

Aunt Sarah looked at me and I nodded. I knew how to play but it seemed better to keep my mouth shut.

'We'll need to teach him then, won't we, William?'

'Not today,' William said flatly, as he finished laying out the chess-men.

I watched the game for some time – they were both much better players than me.

They sat hunched over the board, hardly speaking except to say things like, 'Good move!' or 'Oh dear, I didn't notice that.' It was boring, just sitting there.

I looked round the room. There were photographs everywhere. I got up and wandered round, looking at them all.

'You like my picture gallery, do you, Thomas?' I jumped. I hadn't realized the chess game was over.

'Who are all these children? Are you one of them?' I pointed to a photo of five children and a dog.

Aunt Sarah named each child: 'William, Thomas, Rachel, myself and little David. He was your grandfather.'

'And mine,' added William.

'Yes, of course, and yours.' She sighed. 'And now I am the only one left.'

'And the dog?' I asked, pointing.

'That was Silver. He belonged to Thomas.'

I felt an icy cold breath of air swirl round me as Aunt Sarah spoke. It was very odd – the windows and door were closed so there shouldn't have been a draught. I shivered.

As William put the chess-men and the table away, he threw me a strange look. Fortunately, Mum came to get us just then and we left.

'I've got some other comics,' I said, when we were back in my room. I was doggedly determined to make friends with William.

'You shivered then, didn't you? Didn't you?' he repeated, when I didn't answer. 'So it *has* started, hasn't it?'

I felt myself go pale. 'What do you mean? What's started?'

Mum came in with some cans of coke and some snacks.

William said nothing until she'd gone. 'The ghosts have come, haven't they?'

'William, don't be daft, there's no such thing …'

'But you felt the cold air! You shivered, Tom, didn't you?'

'Yes, well, it was a gust of wind through the windows or the door or the …'

'No, it wasn't. You felt it. It's because your name is Thomas, like I said.' William looked at me. I knew he was trying to scare me.

'Don't be daft! What's my name got to do with it?' I was trying to keep my voice calm.

'I'm not daft – you ask your mum.'

'You said that yesterday. What does Mum know?'

'Aunt Sarah's brother, Thomas, and his dog Silver – they're ghosts, see. Anyone in the family with the name, Thomas, gets spooked by them. Ask your mum.'

I gaped at William. 'You keep saying that.'

'Well, she's seen it happen – when you were a baby.' He finished the last of his drink. 'I'll see you at school I suppose.' He stood up to leave.

'I'm not spooked!' I shouted as he left the room.

'Thanks, Auntie Helen,' he called, and he let himself out of the house.

I wanted to ask Mum about it, but I couldn't. I remembered the way she looked when I talked about the howling dog, and how she hated coming to Ardcardish. Did she believe in ghosts? Was that why she hadn't wanted to come here?

5

The new school

'Mum said I should go with Tom to the headmistress,' William said, when Mum opened the door on Monday morning.

'I want to see Mrs McFarlane,' said Mum, and she came with us. I felt embarrassed. William grinned unpleasantly. When we reached the school gates, William pointed us to the head's office.

Mrs McFarlane spoke to Mum, and then she walked me to my classroom. 'You'll be in Miss Neil's class. That's your cousin's class too,' she said.

'Sit there, Tom.' Miss Neil pointed to the only empty desk – next to William's. 'Stop scowling, William. You and Tom will be working together on our project.'

William stopped scowling but he didn't look too pleased. I wasn't happy about it either.

Miss Neil started telling me about the project the class was doing. '… Ardcardish during the Second World War,' she said. 'William will show you his notes and perhaps you could ask your aunt Sarah Caird if she has any old shop records that we could look at.'

'I'll ask her,' William butted in, before I could even open my mouth.

'It doesn't matter who asks, so long as one of you does.' Miss Neil gave us each a look. 'Now maths. The work is on the board, Tom.'

She turned away and sat at her desk while we wrestled with the work. Apparently, William was good at maths and finished before anyone else in the class. I was last.

But when we had to write a short piece on something we'd done recently, not only was I finished first, but mine was read out.

William was not impressed, and he left me alone at both break and lunch period. No one else spoke to me either, so I spent the time sitting on the wall, enjoying the sunshine.

In the afternoon, we heard sirens screaming as the emergency services rushed past the school. William and I sat near the window.

By standing on tiptoe we could just about see what was happening.

'That was a police car!' William whispered.

'There's an ambulance following it,' I said.

Everyone was standing up trying to see.

'Would you all please sit down!' Miss Neil shouted above the buzz of voices. But she was interested too, and she came over just as the fire engine went by with its bells ringing.

'There must have been an accident further up the glen. I hope no one was hurt. Now let's get on with our geography lesson.'

But each time a car went past, William and I tried to look out of the window. Miss Neil told us off, and somehow that made William a little more friendly.

On the way home, we walked together and he pointed out a jumble of rocks.

'That's Bracken Hill. There's a cave behind those rocks. A landslide blocked it ages ago.'

'Can we go and see it?'

'Maybe, but I've got to collect Margaret from playgroup now. It's big Morag's day off and Mum can't leave the post office.'

'Come in afterwards so you can ask Aunt Sarah about the shop records,' I said.

William ran up the steps of the church hall to get his sister. Not much later, he came in after we'd just finished our tea.

'I suppose you'd better come with me to see Aunt Sarah,' he said.

I felt he didn't really want to share her with me. He knocked on her door and we went in.

33

'Aunt Sarah, do you have any old account books for the shop? We're doing a project on Ardcardish during World War Two,' William explained.

She turned to look at me. 'Are you in on this project too, Thomas?'

'Oh, yes, but William knows much more about Ardcardish than I do.'

'Hmm. Well then, all the old records and account books should still be in the attic. Take what you need, but be careful with them.'

'We will.' William and I spoke together.

'And be careful in the attic – the boxes will be heavy. Get your father to help you, Thomas.'

She gave us each a huge lump of toffee, and we took off to find Dad and to search the attic.

Dad opened up the attic hatch for us. 'There you are. Be careful. No one has been up here for years. I'll rig up some electric light for you in the caravan and you can use that as a study.' Then he left us to explore.

6

Searching the attic

Weird shadows danced on the walls as
William and I moved about, looking through
the old boxes.

I pulled a sheet away from a pile of junk
and raised a cloud of dust. Both of us started
sneezing. Our eyes watered and we rubbed
them, leaving our faces filthy.

I grinned. William looked very odd with his dirty face and cobwebs in his hair.

'Look at yourself.' William grinned back at me. He pointed to a mirror that was propped up against the wall.

I looked a mess too. I stared at our reflections. 'We could be twins,' I said.

'Well, we *are* cousins,' William snorted and turned away.

It took ages, but we eventually found two boxes of account books for the years of the Second World War.

I also found a small brown case with a key tied to the handle.

'What about this?' I showed the case to William.

'Take it,' he said, and he began to push the boxes towards the hatch.

I climbed down the ladder, holding the case, and called for Dad to give us a hand. He carried the boxes, one at a time, to the caravan.

'I'd like to live in a caravan,' said William.

'It's not that great; nowhere to keep books and things.' I put the small case down.

'Still, it would be good.'

'Maybe you could come and stay.'

Dad dumped the second box on the table.

'Thanks very much.' William gave Dad a great broad grin. It made him look quite different. Dad smiled back at him. 'Have a good time,' he said, as he left us.

We had a quick look through the boxes. William arranged the records in date order on the table. But we decided to wait till the next day to examine them properly. Even in the short time we had been inside the caravan, the wind had become much stronger and I found it hard to shut the door. I locked up the caravan and added the key to my key-ring.

From the sitting-room window, I watched the waves roll into the shore; all white tops with the foam blown across the road. It made the windows all streaky.

It was time for bed. My room faced the hill so it was much quieter there and I went to sleep straight away.

In the middle of the night, a sound woke me. At first I thought it was Mum and Dad.

I could hear them moving about. I got out of bed and went over to the window, thinking that perhaps someone was outside.

The same cold gust of air flooded round me as it had in Aunt Sarah's room – but my window was shut tight.

Then I heard it – a frightening sound that made my hair raise at the back of my neck.

I heard a long drawn-out howl. Somewhere out on the hill, a dog was howling.

The sound rose and fell above the noise of the wind. It was the sound I remembered hearing when I was little. Then I remembered William's talk about ghosts.

It was a long time before I slept.

7

Sounds in the night

In the morning, I went to the kitchen feeling tired and heavy. Mum was sitting at the table, white-faced, nursing a mug of tea in her hands. Dad was there too.

'You're late, didn't you sleep well?' Dad asked.

'The wind woke me, but I slept again after a while.' I was about to say I had heard the howling dog, but the look on Mum's face made me change my mind.

I ate in silence.

I remembered how scared Mum had looked the last time I'd told her about the howling dog.

Mum got up from the table and rinsed her mug at the sink. 'You'd better hurry. William has just left.'

I crammed my packed lunch into my bag, put on my coat, and ran, soon catching up with William.

'Did the ghost dog keep you awake?'

'What ghost dog?' I asked, although I knew what he meant.

'The howling on the hill last night.'

'You don't believe in all that stupid stuff do you? It was just the wind.' But I didn't say that I had felt the cold draught again.

'You don't know anything. It has started again because you're here. And it comes from up there.' And William pointed to the jumbled fall of rocks on Bracken Hill, above the end of the forestry road.

* * *

The school bell rang and we were given a black mark for being late. Miss Neil kept us busy all day and William ignored me again during break and lunch.

However, he did walk home with me and I suggested going to look at the rocks. It seemed the only place I could go to get an answer to the mystery crowding in on me, ever since I had arrived in Ardcardish.

'There may be a hole where the wind goes through,' I suggested, hopefully.

'I don't see how. The cave mouth was covered by the landslide.' William stood looking up at the rocks.

'Come on, it shouldn't take long. It's not far.'

William looked as if he was going to say no, then changed his mind. 'All right, but let's be quick,' and he set a fast pace up the forestry road. I had to run to keep up with him.

We climbed, in silence, up to the rocks. I looked at the big boulders that had fallen down the hillside.

I imagined what it must be like to be caught up in a landslide and I shuddered. The rocks had left a tiny gap and I could just make out the rounded top of the cave.

'There *is* a gap here.' I pointed and began to climb up towards it.

'Can you see any …' William's voice faded out in a sort of gurgle.

I glanced back. The freckles on his nose stood out against his white face and his mouth was open. His eyes caught my attention. He was staring at something beyond me. I sensed his fear and went cold.

Turning, I saw on a rock nearby, a large, silvery-grey dog. Its fur was wet.

I could see the pinkish sheen of its skin. Its tongue hung out.

I shivered, feeling cold air swirling round me. Behind the dog, I thought I saw the outline of a boy and another bigger, shaggier dog.

'The ghost dog!' croaked William.
He shrank back, then turned and ran down the hill.

I turned again to the dog. It had vanished!
It can't have been a ghost – it was breathing, I thought to myself.

I climbed to where it had been. Its tongue had been dripping saliva and there should have been some on the rock.

I turned and ran after William.

He was sitting with his back against a post, at the foot of the forestry road.

'What did you go to the rock for?' he said, still out of breath.

'To see if it had left drips from its tongue.' I panted and slithered down beside him.

'Did it?'

'No!'

'Now do you believe me?'

'No, I don' .' I spoke slowly, as I remembered something. 'That dog was real. Remember the dog in the photo of Thomas? It was a deerhound – they're long-coated. This one we saw had a very short coat.'

William looked at me for a minute, but then he nodded. 'OK. You're right. But what about your mum? She used to hear the dog howling when you lived here before. And she's sure that, as a baby, you used to see things that no one else could. I know, because she told my mum that's why you left.

'There were lots of rows because your dad said it was Aunt Sarah's fault, always living in the past and putting ideas in your mum's head. But it wasn't.' He glared at me. 'Don't lie. You *did* feel a cold wind in Aunt Sarah's room, didn't you?'

'OK. I did.'

'Well then, that proves it. There must be a ghost.'

48

I didn't want to agree with him, so I stood up and so did he. 'Your trousers are wet,' I sniggered.

William turned me round. 'So are yours.' We both laughed hysterically until our faces were wet with tears.

Then we stopped as suddenly as we'd started. We stared at each other and ran home.

William's mother was waiting for us on the stair landing. She looked furious. 'Where've you been? What have you been doing?'

She took William by the arm and pulled him inside. Before the door was shut, he gave me a poisonous look.

8

The dog on the hill

Next day, William was ahead of me on the way to school. In the playground, he grabbed me and punched me in the stomach.

'I got into trouble because of you last night. I forgot to collect Margaret from playgroup. It's all your fault.'

'No it isn't.' I tried to pull myself away, but he kept hitting me. I hit back and soon we were both rolling on the ground.

'I hate you. I don't want you here,' William gasped at me.

'I never wanted to come here in the first place!'

Suddenly I felt myself being grabbed.

'William! Tom! Get up! You know we don't tolerate fighting.' Mrs McFarlane pulled William to his feet. 'Who started it?'

Neither of us said a word. We stood there, scowling at the ground.

'Hmmm. Well, go to your class at once.'

We fled. Miss Neil glared at us as we sat down but she said nothing. At the end of the last lesson, she asked me to stay behind.

'I hear that you and William were fighting. What was it all about?' she said.

'I don't know,' I mumbled. And it was true. I didn't know why he hated me sometimes.

Miss Neil looked thoughtful. 'You know his father drowned only months ago in a fishing accident, don't you?'

'Yes, Dad was at the funeral.'

'I think it's hard for William. He misses his father and now he has to share things with you. Do you understand, Tom?' She added, almost to herself, 'And your name doesn't help either.'

I looked at Miss Neil's solemn face and muttered, 'OK.'

Then I turned and ran from the room.

I didn't feel like going home and somehow I found myself on the forestry road. I climbed up to the jumbled rocks and sat on the rock where the dog had stood.

I thought about William, and knew that it would be terrible if anything ever happened to my dad. Maybe it was hard for William. But it was hard for me too.

Everything seemed full of mysteries that made no sense. And yet they all seemed to have something to do with me. Or at least, something to do with my name.

Then I heard a slight whine near me and I looked round.

There was the dog, standing watching me. For a moment I felt scared.

'Hello, dog.' He cocked his head on one side and walked towards me. I could see that he was limping.

'Good boy. You look hungry.'

I took out a left-over sandwich from my
lunch box and threw it to the dog. He caught
it in mid-air and wolfed it down in one gulp.
Then he looked hopefully for more.

'None left, but I'll try and bring you
something tomorrow.' I stood up, hoping
to catch hold of him to read the tag on his
collar. But the dog backed away and limped
off towards the fir trees.

Suddenly, I felt the now familiar cold air round me. By the trees, where the dog had been standing, I thought I could see two shadowy figures: a boy in a long raincoat and a great hairy dog. Was it a trick of the light?

William came for me after tea. He seemed friendly enough and neither of us said anything about the fight. We went down to the caravan and William looked at the account books.

54

Secretly, I thought all the musty old books full of spidery figures were rather dull. I was much more interested in the small case.

Inside were some old photos, copies of the ones in Aunt Sarah's room; an old, stained Bible with 'William Caird' written inside; and a battered old jigsaw puzzle. The last thing was a five-year diary. On the inside page was written:

Sarah Caird
her
special diary
1939

'This is Aunt Sarah's diary, starting on 1st January 1939,' I told William.

'I bet it's boring, probably all about dolls and tea-parties ...' William didn't even bother to look up. 'This is much more interesting.'

I flipped through the pages. William had been right about the tea-parties with someone called Letty. Just as I was going to shut the book, I noticed my name, 'Thomas', on one of the pages. 'It says here, "20th June: Thomas says he saw William going up the hill with a hen under his arm." A hen? What would he want a hen for?' I nudged William.

He looked over my shoulder. 'What else does it say?'

'Next entry, 21st June: "Our cockerel has gone missing. Father is furious. Thomas thinks William took it for cock-fighting. He says the men use the sheep-pen as a fighting ring." I thought cock-fighting was against the law.'

'It is now. I don't know about then.' William peered at the book. 'It says money has gone missing from the till.'

I turned more pages to find the next entry. 'Here it is: "20th July: Father is making us all keep an account of what we spend – even William who is almost grown up."

Then nothing more except that it rained all week.'

I turned the page once more.

'"21st July: More money has gone missing. Thomas and William had a fight. William has such a temper – he cut Thomas' face. I wish I could stop them. I think it is all to do with that stupid money. Thomas knows where it is. He went out – I think to try to find it."

'The next entry is the following day. "22nd July: There was a great landfall last night on the hill. Thomas did not return last night, nor did Silver. Father and William are organizing a search."'

'That's what caused the jumbled rocks,' said William.

As I looked up at him, I felt a cold wind round me. I could have sworn someone was peering in at the window. I tried not to shiver.

William looked at me strangely. 'Is there any more about Thomas?' he asked.

'No, there's no more after that.' I flipped through the book. 'No, wait! "3rd September: We are now at war with Germany. William says he's going to join up as soon as he can." That was the start of the Second World War.'

'William was killed in that war.'

'Yes, it says that here.' I read it out. '"We have had a telegram to say William died at Dunkirk. They are bringing his body home." And very faintly in pencil it says, "I think Thomas and Silver are dead too." And that's all. It seems so sad, doesn't it? And now there's only Aunt Sarah left.'

'I wonder what really happened?' said William.

Mum came and told us that we had better pack up for the night. Soon after she'd gone, William and I locked up the caravan.

I told William, 'I saw that dog again today, at the rocks. It's starving! I'm going to feed it tomorrow. Do you want to come?'

'OK. Morag is picking Margaret up from playschool, so it'll be all right.'

William waved as he went into his own house.

I had a nightmare that night. I was in the middle of a battle and Aunt Sarah's brother, William, was trying to tell me something but I couldn't make out what he was saying.

9

Desperate

The next morning I left money for a tin of
dog food and some large dog biscuits. I even
remembered to take a tin opener and a
spoon.

After school, William followed me up the
hill. When we reached the rocks, I opened
my bag and set out all the food. I opened the
tin and scraped out the meat on to a flat
rock. I kept some of the biscuits in my hand.
I sat down nearby to wait for the dog.

'Aren't you going to put out the biscuits
too?' William sat down beside me.

'I want to catch hold of him, so I'll see if he'll take them from me. I want to see his collar tag.'

We waited in silence, but the dog didn't come. I was just about to get up when William drew in his breath. He was staring towards the fir trees.

There was the dog, limping towards us. He sniffed the air, slowing down to a stop as he neared us. We sat quite still. The dog waited. We waited too.

When he decided we weren't dangerous, he came forward and gulped down the tinned food quickly. I held out a dog biscuit to him.

He came nearer and stretched out his head to get it. I made a grab for the collar.

The dog snatched the biscuit and pulled away. He ran downhill limping, with the biscuit clenched firmly in his teeth.

I muttered angrily under my breath. 'I thought I had him. There's no point waiting now. He won't come back. And it's starting to rain.'

I left the rest of the biscuits on the rock and we went back down the hill.

'I'm not going to say anything about the dog yet,' I said, when we were almost home.

'OK, I won't either, but how are you going to keep feeding him?'

'I've still got some birthday money left.'

That night it rained heavily, and in the morning, Dad drove us to school. He picked us up again at four o'clock.

After tea, the rain stopped for a while and I rushed up the hill to leave food for the dog. The forestry road was awash with water and it was just as well I'd put on my wellies. Even the ground beside the rocks was soggy and my feet sank into the earth.

I put the food down in the same place and waited, but the dog didn't come. It was almost dark when I got home.

10

The jigsaw

On Saturday morning I couldn't see the hill
at all. 'Why doesn't it stop raining?' I asked,
angrily. I thought how wet and hungry the
dog would be.

'It will, it will,' said Mum, as she poured
me a mug of tea. 'You can ask William to tea
tonight, if you like.'

'OK, thanks, Mum.'

She smiled. She seemed a little more
relaxed – maybe she thought I was settling in.

I couldn't go to feed the dog because the weather was so bad – the rain was still bucketing. At home we mucked about a bit, and then William noticed the old jigsaw puzzle from the case in the attic.

'Where's this come from? It looks really old.' William looked at the lid but there wasn't a picture on it. We tried to see if we could fit the pieces together, but it was hard because we didn't know what it was supposed to look like.

Then Mum called us to the kitchen. It was warm and cosy, in spite of the rain battering on the window.

'Auntie Helen, you've made an *everything* pizza! Is it specially for us?' William grinned at her as she gave us huge helpings of food. She looked happy.

We had almost finished when Dad asked, 'Tom, you're first down in the shop in the morning. Who buys all that dog food?'

There was an uncomfortable silence. But there was no point in lying.

'I buy it myself, Dad, with my own pocket money. I found a dog up on the hill, near the fallen rocks and I've been feeding it.'

'Why didn't you tell us?' said Dad, frowning.

'I – I don't know, Dad.' How could I tell him about the howling dog and how William and I thought it was a ghost?

'A dog was lost on Monday, from that accident up the glen. I met the owners today. They're looking for it, now that they're out of hospital.'

'That was the day you started school,' said William. 'We saw the ambulance. Do you remember?'

'I'll give them a ring in the morning,' said Dad, sternly. 'And they'll have to check that it *is* the right dog.'

'This dog has a collar and a tag, but I can't catch him. I must feed him, he's starving,' I pleaded.

But Dad was firm. 'Tom, you must *not* go up to the rocks in this rain. It's dangerous.

68

There could be a land-slip at any time.'

Nothing more was said, and after tea, William and I carried on with the jigsaw. It was a bit boring – just a picture of a hillside with trees and a cave.

We had just finished it when Aunt Sarah tapped on the door and came in. Her eyes brightened.

'Oh, I haven't seen that for years,' she exclaimed. Then she smiled rather sadly. 'Do you know what it is?'

William and I looked blank.

Aunt Sarah clicked her tongue impatiently.

'Use your eyes! Imagine Bracken Hill without the fall of rocks.'

We looked again.

'Of course!' cried William, excitedly. He pointed at the black bit in the middle. 'That must be the cave that disappeared.'

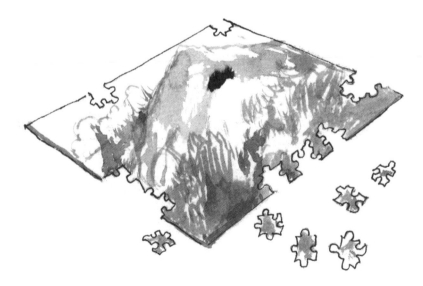

'That's right, William. The jigsaw was made from an old photo taken before the war.'

She looked at me hard. 'And Thomas, please do not go on the hill in this weather. Neither of you! It really is dangerous. I don't want anything to happen to you.'

William and I stared after her as she left the room.

'You're not going up there tonight, are you?' William asked.

'No, I won't go up when it's raining. Dad said not to. But I must feed the dog soon. He'll be starving. I'll go in the morning.'

After William had left, I sat for a while, looking at the puzzle. I kept thinking I was looking at the hill as Aunt Sarah and her brother, Thomas, knew it.

And as I looked at the picture, I felt ice-cold air blowing round me yet again.

'Thomas?' I whispered and looked round. There was no one there. I shivered. I broke up the puzzle and put it away.

Then I gathered together the dog food and
biscuits, and put them in my rucksack along
with the tin opener.

I set my alarm for six o'clock and put it
under my pillow.

11

Landslide!

I fumbled under my pillow to stop the alarm
ringing, and lay for a moment or two,
listening, in case anyone woke up.

I dressed quickly and peered out of the
window. The rain had stopped. I could go up
the hill without disobeying Dad. Picking up
my rucksack, I opened my bedroom door and
crept along the hall. I slipped on my coat and
boots.

I waited on the landing for a few
moments. Nobody looked out.

I ran down the stairs, round the side of the building, and most of the way to the forestry road. It was not properly light yet and I kept tripping over branches and large stones.

After I fell for the second time, I walked on the grass. It was terribly slippery but at least I didn't get any more water in my boots.

By the time I reached the fallen rocks, I was out of breath. I whistled for the dog and for a second, I thought I heard an answering sound.

Curtains of rain began sweeping across the hill and it was difficult to see. I began to wish I'd stayed at home. Then out of the rain the dog appeared.

He came right up to me, wagging his tail. His coat was running with water.

'I've brought your food,' I said. I pushed the dog biscuits towards him, and he wolfed them down while I spooned food on to the rock. He ate some and then he stepped back, whining. He stood with his head raised, as if listening. I listened too, but I couldn't hear anything except the rain drumming down.

'What's the matter, boy?' I asked, but the dog edged away, still whining. He looked at me and gave a little bark.

All of a sudden, there was a rumble like thunder and the rock seemed to move. The dog barked again and ran off whimpering.

The rock, with a blob of dog food on it, slowly began to slide away. I watched in horror as it gathered speed.

Then I was moving too. I tried to jump sideways to get off the moving earth. But I was off balance and I fell over. I struggled to get up but the ground moved faster and faster.

I yelled and tried again to stand. Small branches scratched my face and the water soaked me. I was too scared to call out again. Something heavy hit me on the side of my head and banged my shoulder and arm.

As everything went black, I thought I heard someone shouting.

12

A lucky escape

I felt as if I was swimming towards the light.
I wasn't wet any more, or cold. I opened my
eyes. Mum was bending over me. She smiled.

'Hello! How are you feeling?'

'What happened? Where am I?' I tried to
sit up, but the room seemed to go round and
round. I lay back again with a groan. Mum
leaned over and held my hand.

'Don't try to sit up yet. You're in your own
bed. You had a knock on the head and your
shoulder is badly bruised. Nothing broken, but
the doctor wants you to stay in bed today.'

'What day is it?' I opened my eyes once more and this time I could keep them open.

'Sunday, same as it was this morning. It's lunch time now.' Dad was standing beside Mum.

'You gave us a bit of a fright, you know, Tom.'

Suddenly, I remembered. 'The dog! What's happened to the dog?' I sat up properly.

My head buzzed, but I stayed sitting up.

'The dog's fine. His owners were on the hill looking for him when the landslide happened.'

'Landslide?' I looked from one to the other.

'The hill looks almost like the jigsaw again,' Aunt Sarah said. She was sitting at the foot of my bed.

I leaned back against the headboard and thought for a moment or two.

'How did you know where I was?'

'When I found your bed empty at breakfast time, I asked William. He told me where you'd gone,' said Mum.

'You were very lucky. I went up the hill and found the dog's owners carrying you down,' said Dad. 'They had found their dog and he led them to you. Now it's time for you to have some rest.' He and Mum left the room.

Aunt Sarah sat still for a few moments. I think she was crying.

'Oh Thomas, Thomas, I thought I had lost you too. Thank goodness you're safe.' She got up suddenly and left me alone.

I wondered why she was so upset, then I remembered her brother – the other Thomas. The cold air swirled round me and I snuggled down under my duvet and slept.

13

The letter

Mum brought me a tray with breakfast and a paracetamol. Then William came to see me.

'How are you?' he said.

'OK.' My head had stopped spinning round, and I felt fine.

'When are you allowed up?' William sat down in the creaky chair.

'Tomorrow.' I struggled to sit up. It's amazing how difficult it is when you don't have the use of both arms. My left one was still very sore.

'Let's have another look at that old jigsaw. It's in the case on the top of the wardrobe.'

William sat on the bed, with the table between us, and we finished the jigsaw quite quickly.

'Now the hill looks almost like this again. You can see it from your window.'

I got out of bed to look. The cave was clearly visible. It looked just like the jigsaw, except for a great brown scar of mud all the way down to the forestry road.

Suddenly, I knew how close I'd come to dying up there. I had to find out more about the mystery of that cave. It had something to do with the past – something to do with Aunt Sarah.

I reached up on top of the wardrobe for the case again. Perhaps there was a clue in it. My head started swimming and I fell heavily, with the case on top of me. Everything flew out and papers fluttered all over the room.

'Tom! Are you all right?' called Mum, anxiously.

'He's OK, Auntie Helen,' said William, 'just dropped something.'

We both scrabbled around the floor for the photos and the diary. The Bible had completely come to bits. I could see that the front cover had come away from the rest of it.

'What's that?' A yellowish bit of paper was sticking out from between the outer and inner front cover.

'It looks like a letter.' William pulled it out and opened it up. It was badly stained and very creased.

'I'll read it.' William's voice was almost a whisper. The room seemed to go very cold. A breath of icy wind made the papers flap gently.

'"Dunkirk. I'm getting Charlie, my pal, to write this. I've been hit badly. Do you remember when Thomas and Silver disappeared? I stole money from the till to pay for bets at cock-fighting. Thomas and I had a big fight about it. I was sure he was going to tell Father. I hid the money in a tin, in the cave on Bracken Hill. Thomas guessed it was there, and he went to look for it with Silver. But the landslide happened. I went there but I couldn't hear anyone inside, although I called and called. I was scared but I tried to tell Father about Thomas. He wouldn't listen. I'm glad I've told you now because I'm not going to make it. I'm so sorry. William."'

'And underneath it says, "William was badly wounded in the chest. He died shortly after in the rescue boat." Signed, Charlie.'

We didn't say anything for a while; we both felt so sad.

'Poor William,' said William.

'Poor Thomas, and Silver too,' I said.

We looked at each other. 'Who's going to tell Aunt Sarah?' we said together.

'Tell Aunt Sarah what?' Mum came in with some snacks for us.

I handed her the letter.

When she had finished reading it, she looked up at me. She whispered, 'Oh, the poor, poor souls.' Her eyes were full of tears. 'Where did you find this?'

'In the old Bible. We knew it was William's. It split open when it fell. The letter was inside.'

'Dad will tell her. You two stay here.'

14

Solved!

Dad told Aunt Sarah. Afterwards, he told us
that she'd gone very quiet and whispered,
'All those years ago, I guessed. But I never
wanted to believe it. Poor Thomas!'

Dad also told the police and they went up
to the cave to search for any sign of Thomas
and Silver.

I didn't sleep for a long time. I was
thinking about William's letter. When I did
sleep, I dreamed that the other Thomas and I
were chasing Silver up Bracken Hill.

In the morning, I was up late. Dad was away with Sergeant Mackay.

'Aunt Sarah is having her breakfast in bed this morning,' said Mum. 'She didn't sleep very well. It's all been quite a shock for her.'

Dad came back carrying a rusty old tin.

He went into Aunt Sarah's room. Aunt Sarah kept to her room all that day and neither William nor I were allowed to see her.

Next morning, I was startled to see Aunt Sarah in the kitchen.

'Thomas, William, come with me.' She beckoned us to follow her.

'She looks all right,' I whispered to William. We followed her into her room.

She put an arm round us both. 'Thank you, my dears, so very much for finding William's letter. It has solved the mystery of Thomas. I was sure he was dead. Thomas and I were twins, and I just knew,' she whispered. 'So it has been a relief to learn that he and Silver could not have suffered. Now sit down, and I'll show what was in the tin.'

Aunt Sarah opened an old tin and placed three silver coins on the table.

William picked one up. 'They're heavy. What are they?'

'And they've got a man's head on them.' I picked up one of the others.

'They're half-crowns – they can't be used any more.' Aunt Sarah picked up the last one. 'They are the reason Thomas died, and perhaps William too. Who knows? I'm going to give you one each as a keepsake. The third I shall have made into a pendant for little Margaret.' Aunt Sarah smiled at us.

'Wouldn't you rather keep them for yourself?' I asked.

'No, my dear. You and William deserve them, and I don't want Margaret to feel left out.'

'Thanks, Aunt Sarah. We'll keep them for ever, won't we, Tom?'

I thought, *when I'm grown up, I'll give my coin to the next Thomas.*

* * *

Three days later, we stood beside Aunt Sarah at the family grave, and watched silently as Thomas and Silver were buried. Now they would never be separated.

I don't know why, but I stayed by the grave after everyone left. Suddenly, there was a rush of cold air. I looked up.

Standing on the other side of the grave were two shadowy figures. The boy was about my age. The great deerhound stood wagging its tail. The boy waved and smiled, a funny, half-sad smile. And then they were gone.

I blinked hard. Had I imagined it all?

I stumbled back to the car. And then I realized the cold wind had gone and somehow, I knew that I would never feel it again.

About the author

I have always lived
in Scotland. I live in
Helensburgh with my
husband, in a tall terrace
house with 41 steps up to
the top floor where my
study is. There is a grand
view of the River Clyde.

I keep an 'Ideas Book'
in which I jot down all sorts of information
that might be useful. In it I had some
information about a landslide and another
about someone disappearing and I thought
these might be used to make a ghost story.
I hope you've enjoyed it.